A VIEW FROM CABBAGETOWN

Barbara Elizabeth Mercer

Copyright© 2012 Barbara Elizabeth Mercer

Art, Design, Cover & inside Paintings & Drawings by © Barbara Elizabeth Mercer

Cover Painting Title: LISTENING, CHATEAU, OTTAWA. Collection The University of Toronto Art Centre.

ISBN 978-81-8253-319-6

First Edition: 2012 ₹ 200/-

Cyberwit.net
HIG 45 Kaushambi Kunj, Kalindipuram
Allahabad - 211011 (U.P.) India
http://www.cyberwit.net

Tel: (91) 9415091004
E-mail: cyberwit@rediffmail.com / info@cyberwit.net

No part of this book may be reproduced or transmitted in any form or by any means, electronic, mechanical, photocopying, or otherwise, without the express written consent of Barbara Elizabeth Mercer.

Dedication

To All those living or dead, who have contributed to the inspiration and encouragement of my Poetry & Painting.

Acknowledgements

PHIL OGISON AND JEFF HOWARD - AMOEBA STARFISH SOUNDSCAPES - for an exciting collaboration and performing with me.

KERON D. PLATT - Guest Poet, Author, Playwright allowing my portrait sketch of him to be published with his poem. Master of Ceremonies for handling the sales of my books at my launches.

FIONA McKEOWN/General Manager and staff Arts & Letters Club of Toronto.

JOSEPH SWEENEY, Catering Manager for creating a beautiful ambience in the Great Hall for my launches.

DON McLEOD / Robarts Library, University of Toronto Libraries, for purchasing my poetry collections for the Canadiana Collection Robarts Library.

BARY GRAY Branch Head Parliament, City of Toronto Libraries, for purchasing my poetry collections for the Historical Section.

STEVE YEATES Graphic Designer, Cabbagetown Preservation Association Newsletter, for publishing my poetry.

ARTS & LETTERS CLUB friends and colleagues for their interest and support.

GUEST POETS, LUCY BRENNAN and LEON WARMSKY

for allowing my portrait sketches of them to be placed with their poetry.

JOHANNA SADELMEYER KATZ for her chicken soup, generosity of spirit and love of poetry.

SUZIE PALMER, Australian Author, for her Foreword to 'Rooted In Cabbagetown 2011.

PUBLISHER, Cyberwit.net (India) Dr, Karunesh Agrawal, Managing Editor, Dr, Santosh Kumar Editor, for their patience and guidance, as always.

Foreword

Three hours prior to learning of the existence of Barbara Elizabeth Mercer's book *A View from Cabbagetown*, I was kneeling in a dew-drenched meadow photographing wildflowers and damselflies. From the meadow I walked along a wooded lakeside path, watching as the rising sun turned the water gold. Six swans came in for a landing, and a man preparing his little boat for a fishing excursion looked, from my vantage point, as if he were doing tai chi on the dock. These are the images I brought home with me, writing haiku in my head and then in a notebook. And then I was presented with the opportunity to write this foreword; and then I opened *A View from Cabbagetown* and read in the first poem, "Is there magic - all around you? / In the early morning mists"—and my complete morning was realized by the light of mutual understanding that poetry (or any art) can offer.

How surprising, in this media-saturated, world-wide-webbed, 21st-century existence, to find an artist expressing such an open, childlike sense of wonder. How unusual to find a book of poetry that transports the reader to a place so charming, so magical, and yet so real—a place called Cabbagetown, no less, a place with history and politics and the sadness and sorrow of any human place, and yet a place where the return of spring is celebrated with a forsythia parade and a summer rain is welcomed with dancing in the streets. A written work's sense of place is in the details, and in Mercer's poems these details include evocative street names as well as references to local politics and neighborhood landmarks.

Many of Mercer's poems read like passages one might find in a letter from a friend, relating the events of days both ordinary and extraordinary, from a cool garden breeze to the violence that can make our world seem instantly unrecognizable. Her voice is personable and sincere, welcoming, gracious, and affable. She does not over-indulge in irony. She celebrates. Yes, she writes about the darker side of life, but even in these poems, a subtle transformation takes place. Events that incite protest or move one to mourning or cause pain—events not worthy of celebration—even these become blessings in disguise in a Mercer poem, reasons to celebrate the life we have, the beauty that we know. "Big Fat Mayor" describes a fat-cat politician whose policies threaten the quality of life; this poems ends with the line "Hurrah Toronto"—a reaffirmation of community and the human spirit.

Even personal pain takes on new meaning. In "Wobbly Tooth," Mercer writes

> Was this wobbly tooth
> Reflecting
> Life around me?
> Telling me - be careful
> Be mindful of what you eat
> What you say

"Have respect - for a wobbly tooth's intuition," this poem instructs us. That might be my favorite line in this collection.

In "Quiet Snowy Morning," a stormy Sunday becomes a true day of rest. "We have been waiting for snow / Waiting for the protection / Of the feeling...." How perfect, that word "protection." It is not a word one often finds in poetry, but of course it is exactly what poetry is: protection against bitterness and despair. Mercer does not go to the opposite extreme of creating a fantasy world. This poem celebrates a "dreamer's day," but in none of her poems does she suggest exchanging this life, with all its challenges and setbacks, for a dream. That would diminish dreams, rendering them merely a substitute form of despair. Instead, Mercer offers us a balance. The view from Cabbagetown is of a life teeming with all the joys and sorrows of a rich, fruitful, full existence.

When Barbara Elizabeth Mercer beckons the reader with, "Let me lure you / Enchant you - take my hand," one simply cannot refuse.

"Surrender to what lies hidden," she writes near the end of this poem, "Let Me Enchant You." We do. Mercer does not eschew specific information, and her poems are richer for it. The trees, the cafes, the backyards of Cabbagetown, the streets of Toronto, take shape before our eyes. We gladly step into this world, for it is ours.

—Jean LeBlanc
Newton, New Jersey, U.S.A

Jean LeBlanc is an Assistant Professor of English in, New Jersey, U.S.A. Her poetry has been published in numerous journals, as well as in collections including *At Any Moment* (Backwaters Press, 2010) and *Where We Go* (Modern English Tanka Press, 2010). She edited the anthology *Voices From Here* for the Paulinskill Poetry Project in 2009. More of her work can be seen at www.jeanleblancpoetry.com.

The Author

Barbara Elizabeth Mercer, Author, Poet, Visual Artist, Performer, born Galt, ON, Canada. Subsequent studies: New York, NY, USA, San Francisco, Cal, USA and Toronto, ON Canada where she worked with educational TVOntario, CBC Television, The Saint Lawrence Centre For The Performing Arts The Canadian Opera Company, The National Ballet of Canada and other Theatre groups.

Although her main focus has been painting and visual art, she has been writing poetry since childhood. Her love of poetry, music and art, began early due to parental hereditary influences. As a member of the prestigious Arts & Letters Club of Toronto, made her performing debut in 2004, which gave her courage to continue performing with readings of her poetry.

In 2012 Barbara is fortunate to have a collaboration with the well known musicians Phil Ogison and Jeff Howard of 'Amoeba Starfish Soundscapes' with whom she will perform her reading of 'A View From Cabbagetown' at The Arts & Letters Club of Toronto.

OSLO, NORWAY INTERNATIONAL LITERARY FESTIVAL 2008, Barbara was honoured to be invited by Literary Critic Adam Donaldson Powell and Publisher Cyberwit.net, India, to launch her poetry collection 'SECRETS' with a performance reading to authors, publishers and the public.

Barbara's poetry collections are included in the permanent Canadiana collections of The Robarts Library, University of Toronto and City of Toronto Libraries, Parliament.

Her paintings are included in the permanent collections of The University of Toronto Art Centre, The RobertMcLaughlin Gallery, Imperial Oil and many private international collections.

Member: Canadian Poetry Association, McMaster University,

Tower Poetry Association, World Poetry Association, Presidents Circle, University of Toronto. The Arts & Letters Club of Toronto.

A View From Cabbagetown 2012, is Barbara Elizabeth Mercer's 9th Collection of Poetry. Others are: Rooted In Cabbagetown 2011. CONCERTO For CABBAGETOWN 2010, ECHOES From CABBAGETOWN 2009, SECRETS 2008, LEGACY 2007, SELF PORTRAIT 2006, MYSTIC WILLS 2005. Co-Author WHEN POETS COLLIDE 2007, with Steve Chering, London, UK.

Email: bemercer@sympatico.ca Web: www.barbaraemercer.com www.cyberwit.net UTube Barbara Elizabeth Mercer, Poem For A Piano.

Contents

ACKNOWLEDGEMENTS 4
FOREWORD 6
THE AUTHOR 9
A MAGUS 15
AMAZING MAZE 16
AMBER TREE 18
ANTICIPATION 19
ARS LONGA VITA BREVIS 20
AUTUMN IS HERE 21
AUTUMN'S FLAMING 23
BEAUTIFUL BLACK BEETLE 24
BIG FAT MAYOR 25
BLESSED BEAUTIFUL RAIN 26
CANADA DAY HOLIDAY WEEKEND 27
CANTATA FOR CABBAGETOWN 28
CAVE 29
CELTIC MOON OF WINDS 30
CLEVEREST CROW OF MILLINGTON STREET 31
CNTOWER PEN 32
COMPOSERS 33
CRIME OF - WRITING POETRY 34
CRUCIBLE 35
DEEP FOG 36
DEEP FREEZE 37
DRIVER - TAKE ME TO NO FRILLS 38
DRUMMER BOY 39
ELDER ABUSE 40
FALCON VALENTINE 41
FLIRTING 42

FORSYTHIA PARADE	43
FROST	44
FULL COLD MOON	45
FULL WOLF MOON	46
FULL - FROSTY - BEAVER - MOON	48
GROWTH OF SPRING	49
HEADLINES OF THE DAY	51
HIGGS BOSON PARTICLE	52
HONEYSUCKLE TREE	53
HONEYSUCKLE TREE - BUNGIED	54
HOPEFUL ROMANTIC	55
HORSE TALE	57
IF I COULD UNDO	59
IGNOBLE BULLIES	61
JUPITER	62
LEAP YEAR	63
LET ME ENCHANT YOU	64
LISTENING	66
LOVE	67
MARCH ARRIVES	68
NEVER SPEAK TO STRANGERS IN A PARK	69
ODE TO A BLACK LABRADOR RETRIEVER	71
ODE TO A TOURTIERE	73
ODE TO VINCENT VAN GOGH	74
OISEAU ROUGE CHANTEUR	75
OSLO NORWAY	76
PENDULUM	78
PERIMETERS	79
PHANTOM MIRROR	81
QUIET SNOWY MORNING	83
RAINY DAY	84
RAPTURE	85
RED ADMIRAL BUTTERFLY	86

ROUND TABLE	87
SISYPHUS SOUP	88
SKIER	89
SOFT SOLED SLIPPERS	90
STORM	91
SUMMER IN CABBAGETOWN	92
SYMMETRY	94
TEMPO ADAGIO	95
'THE CONTAINED GARDEN'	96
THE DAY AFTER THE "RAPTURE"	97
"THE IRISH GENTLEMAN"	98
THE RAPTURED	100
TURKEYS	101
URIM AND THUMMIN	102
VENUS MY RULING PLANET	103
WEST WING	104
WHEN VARIATIONS GO ASTRAY	105
WOBBLY TOOTH	107
LILY OF THE VALLEY MUGUET	109
PURPOSEFUL ROBIN	110
SNAIL LOVE DARTS	111

GUEST POETS

LUCY BRENNAN	112
KERON D. PLATT	114
LEONWARMSKI	116

A MAGUS

Is there a MAGUS in your life
Or - has there ever been one?
Do you know a MAGUS now?
Well - I do
Is there magic - all around you?
In the early morning mists
In the full moon - on its way
To light the sky - stars winking - blinking
And never say goodbye?
Do you see the rainbow
After refreshing us - with storm?
Rushing out to get a glimpse
Before its fleeting presence?
Do you hear birds singing
Trees whispering - seas rolling - rivers flowing
Feel the cosmos tingling
Flowers blooming - bells ringing?
Do you hear
The children's laughter - in the music they perform
Cats purring - dogs barking - sniffing
Clicking their paws
On their way to a run in their park
Unleashed and free - to be what they are?
Well I do - there is - forever
The magician - sorcerer - creating - goings on - richness of life
Is there - in your life
A MAGUS?

AMAZING MAZE

Where are we
In the Maze of our lives?
We try to see where our next footsteps
Will lead us
Through the Amazing Maze
Which path to take
To bring us closer to
The successful exit
Journey
Through
The Amazing Maze
We try to trust our instincts
As a bird
Flying south for the winter
Or north to the breeding grounds
We try to listen
To the wind
Which way does it blow?
We are blown about as a seed
In the winds of spring
Hoping to land in fertile ground
We become entangled
In obstacles
False leads
Pit falls which ensnare us
At each turn
Finally breaking free
Trying again
To see the truth

Honest route
To discover our strengths
To trust
Our innate abilities
Our loadstone
Our instincts - polished - honed
To feel our way
With courage - strength
To believe in ourselves
Our destiny for survival
Our legacy
As human beings
With love - devotion - understanding - empathy
To learn
Through our misguided steps
The shape shifters
False profits
Tricksters
Fire breathing dragons
Obsessive - religious fanaticism
Grasping
For control
To stifle our freedom - creative thought
Through
The
Amazing Maze
Yet
Wounded - or not
We walk forward
There is no turning back
Through the
AMAZING MAZE

AMBER TREE

The amber tree
Stands majestically
Magically - tallest - from my lighthouse view
Abundantly magnetic
In autumn leaves - sun shinning through
Amber light - glowing - gold - dots - of crimson
Surrounds
Blue Jays - diving - swooping - looping
Shiny black Crows - clustering
Happily - cawing - bobbing
Cardinals
Cadmium red - flashes
Darting - from branch - to branch
Have taken up the space
Of Robin - in spring
Robin - sweet song
If Canada Geese
Wished to - break chevron formation
There would be
Amber branches
For them to land on
Before all leaves
Have fluttered
To the earth
In a carpet of
Warm - golden - Amber light
From the majestic - magical
AMBER TREE

ANTICIPATION

I search gatherings - voluminous - pink - purple clouds
In early morning pale blue sky
I hear engines - lusty - passionate - music
Jets flying in from global space
To Pearson International
Which one is coming from Europe?
They are flying too high
For me to see even a whisp of jet stream
The beloved is on one plane
If there has not been a change of plans
If there has been no delay
Has he landed - is he smiling sleepily - thinking of me?
Is he caught in crowded passenger
Inspection lines - luggage lines
Are they scanning his eyes - his body for weapons
To see if he is really - who his passport says he is
Is he lined up to declare - treasures he has brought
For me - maybe?
Is he hailing a taxi now - thinking of me?
Or is he speeding into Toronto
To call me?
I hear his deep masculine voice - see his handsome face
I wait anxiously - hopefully
For news of his adventures
Knowledge gained - lessons learned
Decisions made in our favour - to share
In
ANTICIPATION

ARS LONGA VITA BREVIS

ART ENDURES LIFE IS BRIEF

A beautiful thought
Great Art
Should endure
What is Great Art?
Fashions of the times
May like it
At times
Until fashion changes
There are no exchanges
Life is Brief
It ranges
Life depending
On Art
For survival
For food
Inspiration
For living spaces
Obsessive - devotion
There are no exchanges
ARS LONGA VITA BREVIS

AUTUMN IS HERE

October 2011

Early morning Robin songs
Have been replaced
By Blue Jays - Red winged Black birds
On top of cattails
In marshes
Along river banks
In forests
Loud and strident
Cawing for attention
Singing
Bleu de Manganese
Blanc de Titane
Feathers - flying
Winter is coming
Large Iron Oxide black crows
Silhouetted on tops of
Thalo green
Orange and red trees
Bodies bobbing back and forth
Long - black beaks - opening
A harsher song to their mates
Who understand this love message
To winter - and its coming
Canada geese forming
Large chevrons
Weaving - wending
In cool blue skies

To a winter place
Cardinals
Brilliantly
Flashing
Rouge de Quinacridaon
Rouge d' Azo Moyen
CadmiumTeinte
Their song
To Evergreen trees
Soon snow will be flying
On top of fallen leaves
AUTUMN IS HERE

AUTUMN'S FLAMING

Light my - awaiting - flame - dormant
Light my - ready - bonfire - with Autumn's passion
Of fallen - curled
Life's lonely leaves
In sheaves
Here is a match box
For you
Strike a match on its sandpaper side
Cup it in your hands - gently
So wind cannot extinguish
The flame
Here is the kindling
Dried - brittle - saved
Let it settle - tenderly - fondly - into leaves
Watch - joyous - bursting - flames
Smell the wafting aroma
Clouds of smoke in curlycues
Of autumn's burning
Of burning - hopes and wishes
Sent into - blind - blue - faith
Messages to the cosmos
The frothy distant shores
See the colours
Red - orange - yellow - gold
Hear the crackling - feel the vibration
Feel
The music of hopeful Autumn's
FLAMING

BEAUTIFUL BLACK BEETLE

JULY 15, 2011

Hello beautiful black beetle
Traveling up
Honey Locust tree
Beside me
You are large - shining - as coal - reflecting
Your wings folded - display
White markings - clearly distinguishable
Your legs- feet - strong
Finding footing - silently - antlers - probing - guiding
On ladder - raised bark highway - of my magnificent tree
To dome of sky
Fan shaped leaves
Canopy
Shading me
From blazing sun
Your destination
Some would call you scarab
Creator = Christ - in Germany
Creating life - as you roll your ball of dung
From deep within earth to rising sun
Creating earth's fertility
From prehistory - Cultural Entomology - Buddhism - Taoism
Shamanism - Ancient Egypt - Indo-Europeans
India - Iran - Japan - Semitic people's bible
All have worshiped your creativity
What message do you have
For me?
BEAUTIFUL BLACK BEETLE

BIG FAT MAYOR

We have a big fat Mayor
His name is Ford
Who weighs in at 330 pounds
For all to see
On the TV
So Toronto will not get bored
He has big fat ideas
To reduce our city to seed
Which only a bully
Would need to succeed
Closing libraries
Would be one of his deeds
While he spends his time at 'Timies' You see
Education is something he abhors
Which places him
In the company of boars
Now he is on a diet
To reduce his intake of ice cream
At midnight
So he will not look such a fright
Toronto rose up
Has evolved
Protesting
His cuts to services we need
To make our lives worthy
The Arts - Day care - Swimming pools
Ford thought were only for fools
Hurrah Toronto

BLESSED BEAUTIFUL RAIN

July 23, 2011

*Blessed by beautiful - heavenly rain
At last - after days of
Scorching heat wave
Under 'heat dome'
No cathedral is this
Architecture of nature
Not of Christopher Wren's design
Rain - sounding softly - beginning
On skylights
Music of rain - dancing
Running rivulets
Gradually increasing in strength
Until - full - beating downpour
Blessed - beautiful - heavenly rain
Fragrant as the sea
Fills my nostrils
Cooling - refreshing
Parched lips
Parched limbs
Parched leaves
Hard dry earth
Sucking up moisture
Gratefully - relieving thirst
Wind whips trees
Into frenzied - happy - flailing
People - dancing - barefoot - joyously
Steaming streets Umbrellas - not needed
In this grateful gift*
BLESSED BEAUTIFUL RAIN

CANADA DAY HOLIDAY WEEKEND

Friday July 1, 2011

Fireworks could not compete with
The spectacular sky display
On Saturday July 2nd eve
Lightning lit up the world
As far as the eye could see
Striking terror in
Bird and bee
Striking the CNtower
Explosions - spectacular
Bursts of flame - blasting the sky into shards
Darting - jagged - incisions
Spreading veins of fear
Encompassing the heavens
Thunder roiled
Shaking windows - doors
The very earth - trembled
Wind - whipping trees into
Frenzied twisting - turnings
I watched from my lighthouse
Front row box seat
Awe and wonder
Striking deep within me
The power of the gods of electricity
Unleashed
Exposing - a world of deep secrets
Now revealed - no longer hidden in deception
On that unforgettable
CANADA DAY HOLIDAY WEEKEND

CANTATA For CABBAGETOWN

Means it is sung
A song in different movements
With musical accompaniment
This is my song
My hope
For a joyful
Romantic - rhythmic - stroll
A song
With many verses
Many voices
Through the place
We call
Home
In
CABBAGETOWN

CAVE

As I wander through the cave of my
Mind
Making marks on the walls
Scratching symbols in stone
I am alone
In the cave of my mind
It is my place
Wondering from niche to niche
Reading what has gone before
In this strange - yet familiar place
Making pictures with words
Paintings with colour
Which some may - in the future
Be able to read - to understand
As a primitive need
To make a mark
To light a spark
To show me the way
To the opening of light
Which propels me forward
To the entrance and exit
Of the
Cave
Of
My mind

CELTIC MOON OF WINDS

March 8, 2012

March Full Moon
When winds
Sweep the old away
Those who betray
Swept away
By
Celtic Moon Of Winds
Refreshing winds
Bring in a new day
New adventures
Poised
To play
Angry tigers
Blown away
Did not know how to play
When
Happy fish
Find a flowing river
To frolick
To spawn
Under
CELTIC MOON OF WINDS

CLEVEREST CROW OF MILLINGTON STREET

While trundling
My shopping buggy
On my way home
Along Millington Street
"millionaires row'
Suddenly
A large black shiny crow
Flapping his wings - cawing loudly
Demanded my attention - teasingly
'Look at me
I am at the top of the
Millington middle house
On the roof
Watch me!
Look what I have found
In my private treasure
Securely protected
In an eve trough
I will pick it up in my beak
Look!
It is gold - flashing in sunlight
Could it be - A GOLD DUNHILL LIGHTER?
Are you not
Amazed by my cleverness?'
Yes! I am! - Yes! I am! I replied - laughing
To the
CLEVEREST CROW OF MILLINGTON STREET

CNTOWER PEN

The CNTower is a pen
A writing pen
Of multifaceted impressions
It reaches for highest ideals
It writes on early morning mists
It writes on the sunrise
With golden script
It writes on the night sky
Reaching for the moon
Reaching for the stars
With red - green - silver - gold - flashing - flourishes
With delicate point
Dipped in
The hopes and wishes
Of the multicoloured city
It gathers my thoughts
Before dawn
It accepts my mantra
Decodes
Spreads in waves
To the four corners of the cosmos
Into the heavens
Sings - with full orchestral - love poem
A concerto to the universe
The CNTower is
My inspiration
My landmark - my harbour
My golden pen

COMPOSERS

There are composers
Whose compositions cover
All situations
With varied postulations
Their fingers are fleet
At any keyboard
They find a seat
Making soundscapes
Of poetry
Passionately - tenderly
Ebony keys - Ivory keys
From deep bass to bell-like treble
Makes one tremble
You will be lucky to meet
These composers
As they are rarely at home
Though you may find them
Wandering the world
Strolling imaginations
Receiving blessings
From the muses
These clever composers
Really exist
Are not a myth
But really remarkable
COMPOSERS

CRIME OF - WRITING POETRY

Yes I am guilty - I admit freely
The crime of writing poetry
When I do not know the proper forms
When I am most uneducated
Yes I am guilty
Please forgive me
Have mercy
Make my sentence humane
Do not shun me
In that I cannot stop the flow
Of words
Which demand my recognition
My cognition
My ignition
To light the sparking
Explosion
Words which give a description
Allow me no hesitation
Demand personification
Do not wish to be hidden
Under my hats of disguise - rotation
But awakened
With full body formation
Whole and as complete
As if they were heard to speak
Yes I am guilty - of
The crime - of writing poetry
Please do not sue me!

CRUCIBLE

January 14.2012

Living - CRUCIBLE
Heating - to melting point
Assumptions - pretensions - foregone conclusions
In the vessel
Of words
Of music
Concentrated forces
Interacting
Causing
Influence
Change
Development
The years - of boiling
Sometimes - flaming - experience
Before - explosion - implosion - finally
Finale
Broadening - outlook
A new path - to venture - adventure - new rhythms
Pricking - cooling - bursting - hissing
Of piano - bubbles
Music - rumbles - stumbles
Words fumble - tumble - into display
Now - sweet - fragrant - truth - emerges
Slowly - confidently - unhesitatingly
For all - who wish - to view
The production - on screen - as seen
Offering - of - living
CRUCIBLE

DEEP FOG

DECEMBER 21, 2011

Deep pearly Fog
Obscures my lighthouse view
Obscures the giants of commerce
Bay Street
The CNTower
Visible only
Are the roof tops - gardens
Black branched - trunks of leafless
Trees
Waiting for winter to arrive
Hoping for a clear view
Shrouding
Minds
Of the confused
Disillusionment
Held behind
Hidden agendas
From those we trusted
With our futures
Perhaps the rain - Ice storms
Predicted
Will cleanse the air
Of this
DEEP FOG

DEEP FREEZE

January 15, 2012

Half moon
Shines brightly
Into my early morning room
Through frosty air
Palest blue - of clear sky
Pale pink horizon
Reflects sun rising
With sparkling glass
From newly built condominiums - cells of the city
From monoliths of Bay Street
On the surface
Toronto looks clean this morning
Roof tops freshly bathed
In white snow
Our spirits are gladdened
For a new day - for new music
Hopeful - horizon - softly approaching
Thoughts of political struggles
Human angers - climbing ladders - jealously
On bent shoulders of the depressed - oppressed
Religious intrigues
Failing Euro
European disasters - American disasters
Are far away
For a few moments
In this
Minus 15 degrees
DEEP FREEZE

DRIVER - TAKE ME TO NO FRILLS

I NEED A HOTDOG

Something which reminds me of
Summer - festival afternoons
Listening to the band
In Riverdale park
Sitting in the front row
Eating a hot dog
Juicy - embellishments - spilling - From both ends
Golden mustard - emerald green - sweet pickle relish
Iridescent - glowing - shimmering - onions
To the sounds of um pa pa - brass tubas - French horns - flutes
Children's laughter - my laughter
Fragrances of many barbecues - steaming
Smoke rising in joyous configurations
Wafting over Cabbagetown
I need the simplicity - of
A hot dog
Of childhood wonder - awe
Freedom to dance
Not caring who is watching or listening
So
Driver - Take me to No Frills
Where I will buy the ingredients
To remind me of
Summer - festival afternoons
Listening to the band
In Riverdale Park

DRUMMER BOY

DRUMMER BOY
Title of
Delightful collage construction
By artist - unique - extraordinaire
Keron D. Platt
Stalwart member of
The Arts & Letters Club of Toronto
To be added as the third of his works
To my collection
Now he has his wall
His creations
Hanging on Sackville Street
In Cabbagetown
The piece makes me smile
As well as the others
Although it was 'rejected'
For peculiar reasons
Known only to jurors of special summer selection
The Arts & Letters Club of Toronto
I am grateful and give appreciation
For the gift of this 'rejection'

For Keron D. Platt with love.

ELDER ABUSE

What is the excuse
For
ELDER ABUSE?
Bullies - cowards - liars - cheaters
Pretenders - scoundrels - thieves
Greedy - grasping - evil doers
Political - Bunglers Bane - shelf fungus
Religious fanatics - quacks
Weak of brain and - mental power - energy suckers
Use weight - height - physical strength
Gender
To abuse
Weakened
ELDERS
To steal wisdom
Property - connections
Which they believe
Will buy them respect
To feed their needy habit
Of
ELDER ABUSE
Not smart enough - to see the future
To realize
One day - when they are - weakened
Unprotected
They will suffer the reverse affects
Of
ELDER ABUSE

FALCON VALENTINE

February 14, 2012

From my garden window
A surprise!
Suddenly appeared
The spread of wings - 30 inches in length
Flew to a branch of my wounded Honeysuckle tree
He landed in such a way - I had a perfect view
He knew - I was watching
He knew - in myth he is "A light which shines in the darkness"
A protective guardian
He was a - Gyrfalcon - Rusticolus
A Raptor
His flight - more buoyant
Than a Peregrine Falcon
His length 24 inches
He stayed - the Falcon with the eye of Horus
Turning his head to look at me
His wings folded on his back
Were white banded
His eyes - jet black - twinkling
His beak - short - pale yellow
His song
A series of short KAKs
He sang to me
HAPPY VALENTINES!!!!
I AM YOUR GIFT FROM THE SKY
Because he was - you see
FALCON VALENTINE

FLIRTING

Flirting - the lost art
Flirting is subtle
Flirting is fun
Flirting is open
To unlimited possibilities
To vast horizons
To explorations
To dreams
To excitement
To many possibilities
The Flirter
Is a challenger
To those who are stiff - as starch - to march
Frightened - timid - terror stricken
What would others think?
I might be
Discovered
Unwillingness to openness
To be closed off
Restricted
Enjoyment
Flirting is throwing a pebble
Into an ocean
A message in a bottle - destined
To be released - sometime - somewhere
To become the art - of freedom of
FLIRTING

FORSYTHIA PARADE

MAY 6, 2012

First - I heard the drummer's drumming
Leading the
Forsythia Parade
Down Sackville Street
In front of my home
Then - I saw them
Children - mothers - fathers
Grand mothers - grand fathers
Wheeling grandchildren in strollers - buggies
All happily parading
To celebrate the
Forsythia Festival
Annual event in
Cabbagetown
Forsythia branches - waving
Flags waving
Emblazoned - with passionate causes
A colourful sight to see
George Rust-Eye
Local Historian - photographing the event
End of parade
Followed - for protection
A white police cruiser
All will arrive safely
At the celebration
Of the Forsythia Festival
With the
FORSYTHIA PARADE

FROST

October 30, 2011

There is
FROST
On the pumpkins this morning
Carved pumpkins
With Jack Frost hats
Ready to scare
Trick & Treaters
Tomorrow - All Saint's Eve
Frost on rooftops
Of Cabbagetown
Jack Frost danced
Through the night
Making his happy art
He has waited - longing to express
His frosty view
Of creation
His breath - spreading
Beautiful - mysterious - mystical - designs
Of Old Norse
Creation Myth
Odin's birth
The sun is up
Frost illuminating - the way for
Our imaginations
To explore
With fascination - awe
Wonders of the nature of
FROST

FULL COLD MOON

FULL LONG NIGHT MOON
December 10, 2011

As I gaze at you
Through lace - bare - black - winter branches
Making Runic symbols
On your brilliant face
Trying to decipher
Your message to me
A profile portrait is sculpted
Strong - sure - proud - true
Committed to
Shining bright
A diamond shape appears
Runic symbol
Inguz
Completion of cycle
Fulfillment
New idea
Fertility
Through all obstacles
As carrara marble
Reveals its heart
Shimmering light
In darkest
FULL COLD MOON
FULL LONG NIGHT MOON

FULL WOLF MOON

January 9, 2012

First Full Moon 0f 2012
Mysteries to be solved
FULL WOLF MOON
How the wolves do croon
Haunting - lonely - longing
Echoing
Bouncing
To the moon
Back - again - to shadows
Elongated
Runic symbols
Punctuated with
Blinding - light
Illuminating
Fractures
Cracks in leafless walls
Expectations
Fruitless
Endeavours
Destruction of beauty
Thoughtless actions
Disengagement
From Nature's abundance
FULL WOLF MOON
How the wolves do croon
Penetrating
Emotions

Penetrating beneath
Thin - shivering - skin
Fast moving to fruition
Completion
A new cycle begins
New destinies
Full creativity
Not to be impeded
Held back by insecurity
Fearless
Forward
FULL WOLF MOON
We hear your croon
None too soon

FULL - FROSTY - BEAVER - MOON

NOVEMBER 10, 2011

Hello
Full Frosty - Beaver Moon
What is your message for me?
You will not let me sleep
You are bright - phosphorescent white
Illuminating my lighthouse
In the sky
Shining through the world
My sleepy eyelids
Into my innermost - wings of dreams
Your music is the wind
Whipping trees
Twisting violently
Leaves
Cannot hold on to their branches
Are being driven
Into mass migration
Landing in bunches - mounding
On rooftops
Against fences
Into hidden corners
You have revealed to them - and to me
Appearing as richly coloured
Flocks
Swooping - flying - twirling - swirling
In your
FULL - FROSTY - BEAVER
MOONLIGHT

GROWTH OF SPRING

MAY 23, 2011

Growth of Spring
Is sweet
With
Healing scents - exotic aromas - intoxicating
With
Lilly of the valley
In voluminous clusters
Spreading
Finding new spaces to conquer
Violets
Inter mingling
With ancient bricks
In bouquets
Ready for plucking
For a lover's gift
Magnolia blossoms
Spreading a carpet on
Moist - receptive earth
Cherry - pink - passionate blossoms
Inviting bees to bury deep
In their pollen
Holly's delicate white flowers
Stars reflecting
In captured pools
Soft green foliage
Trees
Spreading in the wind

The spring rain - cleansing - polishing - gleaming
Love is in the air
Birds singing their sweetest brilliantly coloured
Compelling - mating songs
It is the time
Of
Awaiting
Expecting
Knowing
Recognizing
Their place
Of Conception
Of propagation
In
This beautiful - enchanting - ecstatic - romantic
Enraptured
GROWTH OF SPRING

HEADLINES OF THE DAY

MAY 24, 2011

The Doomsday people
Disappointed at having
Spent millions
On billboards
To advertise
The end of the world
Their faith shaken
To the core
Ridiculed
Making their own 'hell on earth'
Riddled with embarrassment
That the world did not end
On May 21st, 2011
According to their ancient bible thumpers
Have now postponed
The end of the world
Until
October 21st, 2011
When there will be
Another
'Rapture'

With a chuckle - a smile
We can now breathe a
Sigh of relief
Of course!

HIGGS BOSON PARTICLE

December 14, 2011

"HIGGS run"
Particle physics
The physicist's dream
Hunting for thirty years
To prove how our earth was formed
Some call it the "God Seed"
Knowledge we need
To dispel the myth
Of the man in they sky
Who condemned the human race
To "sin" - "damnation"
That which has
Given false priests
Popes
Hopes
Of filling their coffers
Through control
Domination
Fear
Intimidation
Placing the burden of guilt
As a cross
For us to bear
Until we die of
Distraction
Frustration
Forced - Non-thinking

HONEYSUCKLE TREE

December 7, 2011

Sad little honeysuckle tree
Cut away from strong embrace
By unthinking hands
It once stood proud and tall
Beside my garden window and wall
Pink blossomed bursts
In spring - sweet perfume
Now the stronger half is gone
Its weaker half
Leans to the ground
Is propped up
By a metal stand
Leaning against a cast iron urn
I try to save it
From extinction
With a string of tiny lights
It cannot provide the same
Protection
From prying eyes
For my once beautiful
Jungle garden
It was once my proudest possession
Sad little
HONEYSUCKLE TREE

HONEYSUCKLE TREE - BUNGIED

Mature - standing tall
Gentle - sweet blossoms
Drew birds - to feast in spring
Now wounded
Tied up with a bungie cord
To a bare wooden fence
With wounded vine
Struggling to survive
Diminished of its former self - size
Cut apart
Ravaged
By thoughtless
Foragers
Perhaps
With tender care
I can help it
Survive
Outside my kitchen window
In my small
Green garden
Sanctuary
For birds
And my
Pleasure
HONEYSUCKLE TREE

HOPEFUL ROMANTIC

The old term
'Hopeless Romantic'
Does not apply to me - anymore
As such
This will not be part of my vocabulary
Or my daily life
What has changed my mind?
Recognition of love - there is - Romance
For nature's magnetic pull
In all its beautiful forms
In this harsh time of
Rudeness - thoughtlessness
Lack of good manners
Lack of respect
Lack of courtesy
Lack of consideration for
Others privacy
Others lives - property - struggles - accomplishments
Lack of humanity
Where anger - hatred - envy - uncouthness
Where hospitality is demanded
Then - taken for granted
Where greed is rampant
With never a 'Thank You'
Where protocol - diplomacy
Has not been learned - is ignored
Where pinched nosed pretenders
Try to force
Their unhappy lives on us

As such
For self preservation
Dressed in soft armour
I dwell in a state of
I Am an
HOPEFUL ROMANTIC

HORSE TALE

Halloween 2011

Memories of hometown
Galt/Cambridge
Horse breading town
Jumpers loved and nurtured
Beautiful horses - Jumping at fair grounds
Long Saturday walk
To farm on Blair/Doon Road
Riding a horse
Felt the joy - strength
Of aged - eyes of wisdom - glorious - tender horse
Responding to my reins
A freedom from sadness
As I rocked - sideways - up and down
Learning not to fall off
Or hurt this magnificent new
Fleet of foot - friend
Now Halloween
A precious gift
From a dear - generous friend
A carved wooden - mannikin horse
Replicated from an ancient Chinese horse mannikin
With moving legs - hooves - neck - head
Large in form and spirit
Smoothly polished body - of mellowed blonde
A Palomino - without a tail
I made a tail for it - with unravelled white string
As in a wick from a candle

As I unravelled each fine strand
I was unravelling - streaming
The almost forgotten memories - the mysteries
Of a long lost childhood
Some joyous - some painful
Along the banks of the Grand River
He now had a thick - fine - full - pale tail
I named him
Blair Doon
As he strides - trots - gallops - canters - jumps
On smooth - white marble surface
The coffee table
In his new stable
Now this humble poem
HORSE TALE
For Nancy & John Embry

IF I COULD UNDO

If I could undo
All the mistakes I have made
If I could repair
All the hurt I have caused
All the pain I have inflicted
Unknowingly
All the misconceptions
I was indoctrinated to believe
Would I be
A perfect human being?
Not likely
I am a 'naive'
I have wanted to please
I have wanted
To save the world
From itself
You see
I have wanted to right the wrongs
Of the throngs
Including my most grievous wrongs
If I could heal the wounds
I cannot see
I have turned my gaze on beauty
On nature
Too wild - too - unpredictable
In its efforts
To teach me
To be nonjudgmental
To listen - to see

The world spinning
The way it should be
If only I could undo all the mistakes
I have made
Would I be
A better human being?
Not likely

IGNOBLE BULLIES

Bullies are not noble
Bullies rob ones table
Rob ones empathy
They were not taught
Respect
For others
For themselves
Bullies
Are the insecure - sad beings
Of the human race
Who wish to find a place
Yet not know
How to achieve it
To receive recognition
Without intimidation
Without humiliation
Without violence
In their presence
What lessons must they learn
To become
Noble human beings?
Rather than
IGNOBLE BULLIES

JUPITER

JOVE - JEUDI - GIOVEDI - JUEVES
June 6, 2011

Welcome back
JUPITER
We have not seen you since 1999
You begin your 12 year cycle
Of joy - happiness - health
You are Lord of heavens
Provider of
Fertilizing rains - lightning - thunder
Winds to blow
Dark storm clouds to form
In many magnificent - multifaceted - mingling
Sculptured - in your imagination
Your Halo
Adrastea - Metis - Amalthea - Thebe
Your gossamer rings
Spreading swift legends
Determining the course of our affairs
Made known to us by
Flight of birds
Mystical signs in the heavens
You are the Lucky Planet
Making our lives jovial
Refreshing - beginning anew
Adventures - hinting at
Long hoped for - wishes fulfilled
Welcome back
JUPITER

LEAP YEAR

February 29, 2012

LEAP YEAR has arrived again
When in times past
Every lass
Could propose marriage
To a recalcitrant
A man she thought would be
A good provider
An amazing lover
On bended knee - as Saint Bridget
Asking for the hand of Saint Patrick
The lackey - slacky
Thought to hold the key
To eternity
He fled in fright
Into the night
A lucky night - for Saint Bridget
As it undoubtedly - would have ended
In a spectacular - fidget
LEAP YEAR in our times
When youthful maidens
Forced to relieve
Their parents plight
Were allowed to make advances
To young men
At dances
Furtive glances - suggested advances
LEAPERS took their chances
On LEAP YEAR night

LET ME ENCHANT YOU

Let me lure you
Enchant you - take my hand
We shall walk
Into my cool green garden
Abundant with dreams - imaginings - longings
Abundant with soft sounds of summer
Warm zephyrs
Caressing our smooth skin
Floating - filtering - shimmering - singing - leaves
Velvet - verdant - shadings
Above us
Alizarin crimson cardinal
Serenading our pleasure
Ancient trees in fullest finery
Singing - clear crystal - fountain
Lending music to sweet summer's wonder
Casting diamonds - pearls on gently rippling water
Fingers touching keys of joy
Refreshing - cooling
Fires of desire
Calming - verdant - voluptuous
Honey locust - feathery fans - caressing - our thoughts
Come lie with me
On soft down - pungent - mossy earth
Be with me
No one can see beneath our enchanted canopy
Fragrant - whispering evergreens
Let me enchant you - take my hand
We shall walk

Into my cool green garden
Be with me
Surrender to what lies hidden
Deep within - ardently - questioning - hearts
Until smiling moon and stars depart

LISTENING

Learning to listen
Quietly
Egoless - open - accepting
Listening
To the music of Life - cries - strife - tremblings
Sweet - bittersweet
Colours of life - earth
Sounds - rhythms
Of nature - humming - breathing - singing
Listening to - signs - songs
In isolation
Which guide - heartbeats
Without
Preconceived notions
Brainwashed conclusions
Listening to
Feelings - warnings - protections
Feeling - vibrations - empathy
Deep in the souls
Of the living
The dead
Sorting out - cacophony
To find
The right path - understanding
To follow - fearlessly
To
LISTENING

LOVE

'Love curves its way through life,
Not angular
Not straight arrows to the heart
But on the wind of chance'
The fear of it
Makes some - grumpy - grouchy - greedy
Cross - angry - needy - cranky
Demanding - perfection
Thrashing around - in protective mode
Remembering the hurt they suffered
The unrequited of the past
It gouges deep
Closing off their hearts
Wallowing in their misery
Wounding others in their
Self deception
Not allowing for a fresh perception
The fun is gone
There is only deception
Then it is too late
To change the first impression
That may have been
For a moment in time - more than
A grand illusion of
LOVE

MARCH ARRIVES

March 1, 2, 3, 2012

March - marches in
Throwing its weight of wind
Sweeping - dead wood away
Howling - destroying
Anger - blazing
Furor - amazing
Sweeping - everything - in its path
Into submission
Trees breaking
Shreiking
Twisting
Uprooted - where they once stood - anciently tall
Broken limbs - screaming - strewing
Shingles flying
Roofs - shuddering
Bricks - trembling
Slabs of signs - flying
Falling from skyscrapers
No chance of sleeping
Heavy fisted banging - howling
Sending fear
Of no escaping
Far and near - when
MARCH ARRIVES
Marches in - repeating
A history
Of destruction
Devastation - cleansing

NEVER SPEAK TO STRANGERS IN A PARK

Mercer New York, NY 1963
A park on 23rd

The drawings I did
All those years ago
Of a sad man
Sitting on a park bench
At the end of 23rd
Have mysteriously
Returned
Through the internet
By someone named Richard Hildebrand
"This may be a wild goose chase, but is this your work?"
Yes, it is my work! May I ask how you acquired them?
His explanation - "Old neighbour moving to senior residence,
my wife sorting his things, found them.
The drawing
Chess Player - Washington Square
A smiling man - smoking a pipe
Memories flooding back of those early days
In New York
The adventure - studying Rembrant drawings
Teaching myself to draw well with sepia pen and ink
Doing portraits at
O'Henry's Restaurant in Greenwich Village
Selling my drawings to Ed Spires, ex Franciscan monk, owner
Fabulous Fakes Antique Reproductions
On 2nd Avenue
Being hired to paint and finish

Museum Reproductions
The gods were - and are - kind to me - in my struggle - joy to Survive
as an artist
I am eternally grateful and give thanks
My work has found it's way back to me!
If only as the copies I made
On my iMac OS X Leopard computer.
Barbara Elizabeth Mercer 2 - 12 - 2012
a
Sometimes it pays to speak - despite the warning
NEVER SPEAK TO STRANGERS IN A PARK

ODE TO A BLACK LABRADOR RETRIEVER

My noble hearted
Black Labrador Retriever
His name was Charlie
Dark sparkle - of all knowing eyes
From the moment our eyes met
A truer bond than I had ever seen
Held in his proud head - held high
Nose always to the winds of change
Always my protector
Always knew
Who had good intentions
Or - bad vibrations
Whom I should be wary of
Or - whom - I should believe
Sorting out kind - generous - spirits
From those who had evil intentions
When I seemed - trusting and blind
With those - who were thieves
His coat was coal black
Thick - shine - soft as silk
In sunlight - had a blue sheen
He was large in body - in spirit
Running - fast as lightning - jumping - to greet
His bark was a warning signal
To those who would intrude - those who would harm
His warmth comforted me
His gentleness - loyalty - unsurpassed
Is always what I need
We frolicked in green fields - forests - in summer

Sailed our silver canoe on blue shimmering water
He sang - while I played the piano
Skied in winter - breaking trail
Charlie was - in the lead
Free as the breeze
My nature teacher
My protector - my Noble Hearted
LABRADOR RETRIEVER

ODE TO A TOURTIERE

January 2012
For Wendy Edwards, Daniel et Daniel

Baked to perfection - double golden crust
As I tenderly lifted it from the oven
Filled with
Savory pork
Beef
Onion
Cinnamon
Cloves
Allspice
Mashed potato
Garlic
Herbs
Divine aroma
Filled my home
To celebrate
A New Year
Mouthwatering - warming hearts
Surprise
For a joyful
New Year
2012
I could hear the spirits
Of this old house - past - present
Clapping - laughing - with glee
While they were
Salivating
With expectation

ODE TO VINCENT VAN GOGH

The sky is clear - deep - Thalo blue
Awakened by the fullest moon
Bathing me - in brightest heavenly hue
Excitement draws me to my windows in the sky
Many stars - sparkling - spangled
Capture my eye
I think of you
Vincent Van Gogh
Did you see the same stars
Returning once again?
Suddenly surprised by a shooting star
Rushing - blazing by
What wish shall I make - to reach afar
Will it carry my thought
To a distant shore
Or will it circle the vastness?
Is it a star I have wished on before
Returning to let me know
It is still my messenger?
Having carried my wishes afar
Having made the contact - I wished for
Coming back with brave news
To my connecting point
To pick up another of this dreamer's wish
And begin its journey once more?
To carry to a far shore
SHOOTING STAR?

OISEAU ROUGE CHANTEUR

Crimson Bird Song
March 7, 2012

Sweet mating song
Echoes through my jungle garden
Announcing
Spring
A flash of crimson
Streaks to the small pond
Leaves - still floating
Ice beginning to depart
Water is cold
Cardinal
Does not mind
Dancing around the stone edge
Testing the water with his
Fine claws
Dips his bright red head
Into silent surface
Flaps his wings
A spray
Sparkle - bubbles
His spring bath - again and again
His preparation
For mating
Attracting
The female of his choice
To build a nest
To raise a family - handsome
OISEAU ROUGE CHANTEUR

OSLO NORWAY

July 20, 2011

SHOCKING!!
Terror attack
OSLO
The seat of the Nobel Peace Prize
Bomb - blowing up Government buildings
Centre of Oslo
This gentle - kind - hardy country - Norway
Friend of Canada
Cultural exchanges
Northern alliance - empathies
We are similar
Peace loving countries
Street where I stayed - performed in large white tent
In the park on the Main Street
To an audience of writers - publishers - archivists
Interested public appreciation
At the launch of my poetry collection
'SECRETS'
While guest poet
Oslo's First Literary Festival
My thoughts go to many friends
I made there in - OSLO
Canadian Embassy
Cultural Attache
Bjorn Petter Hernes
His quietly penetrating eyes
Enticingly - willing me

To turn around - I shall never forget
His greeting - hospitality - A cafe
To myself - my publishers from India
Dr. Santosh Kumar Editor
Karunesh Agrawal Managing Editor
Cyberwit.net
Literary Critic - Adam Donaldson Powell
Who wrote the review/foreword
To my book
Store du Verdon's Eli Borchgrevink and others
Generously providing our lunches - dinners
In fine Oslo restaurants
During the festival seminars
Salmon - best in the world
Tronsmo Book Store
Where my book was displayed in the window
My first famous book store in the world
Friendship with International poets - writers
Musicians
The musician - stranger
Who gave me an ice cream cone - his tragic story
In the park
The river with bronze sculptures on the banks
Sailing ships - small and tall - moored in the harbour
Cruise ship waiting to be boarded
Sculpture Garden - rose beds - fragrance upon entering gates
Autumn in OSLO
Memories abound - emblazoned
On my heart
Today - and always
OSLO

PENDULUM

Good morning
PENDULUM
I hear your clicking - ticking
I hear your whirring - it is a song
I hear your buzzing in both ears - cheering me on
Which way will you swing today
Will you be balanced
On your string - or golden chain
Centered in a ring - with miracles to bring
Moving from side to side - never scoring the surface
Darkness and Light - safely above
Fear and Flight
Peace then war
Taking me to the heights
Then plummeting
My naivety in gravity
For ever more
Or will you explore
The edges of my world
Twirling me around - on frenzied ground
In my imagination
Ever expanding
Ever learning - struggling - releasing the pre-conceived
To - understanding
As you have always done
Before?
I am willing - I am open - Good morning
PENDULUM

PERIMETERS

When we are sure
We are secure
When what we have nurtured
With loving care - struggle - without help
Over many years
Built a - green - garden - sanctuary
For our dreams - wishes - hopes
With nature's help
With nature's ecosystem
All is lush - beautiful
Peaceful - healing - after loss of a beloved
When creativity - is free to take flight
With birds alight - on branches
Above one's - happy head
A healing green - summer retreat
Seems the time to invite
Thoughtless - destruction
By other than one's own hand
Invasion - of one's
PERIMETERS
When one day - we are not there
To guard our
PERIMETERS
When did they believe
Your sanctuary
Was theirs?
Find it necessary
To destroy
To inflict a deep wound

On one's happiness
Sneaking - stealthily
So as not to be seen
To do damage
To inflict pain
Without permission
On blossom trees
Climbing vines
With clutching - grasping
Disrespectful
Controlling
On which they are so keen
Trust is broken - gone - the end
Never to return
To one's
Inspirational
PERIMETERS
Which one tries to build again
With hired gardeners
This time
For I am aging
Gardeners who strengthened
Perimeters
To make my garden
Beautiful once more
PERIMETERS

PHANTOM MIRROR

Phantom mirror
Has witnessed much - we know little
Previous houses
Of Grandeur
Social intercourse
For better - or worse
Lives lived - in dark Victorian homes
Where decisions must be made
To stay or leave - laughter - tears
Their first meeting
Greeting - realizing
Their images together - confirming - love - loyalty
Standing before it
As it stood on the floor
In the 'World's Oldest Book Store'
In the village of Green River
Victorian fireplace mantles
Demanded
Magnificence
Attendance
PHANTOM MIRROR
Filled the space - to high ceiling
Reflection - many faceted - crystal chandelier
Reflected - struggles - reflected love
Hung - highly - above
Reflected - grand piano - played with passion
Music imbued - ornate golden frame
It echoed
Mysteries

Hauntings
Happiness
Sadness
Past - present - heartbeats
Will you repeat - what you have seen?
Will you reveal the future?
PHANTOM MIRROR?

QUIET SNOWY MORNING

Sunday, February 12, 2012

Awoke to a blanket
Warm - softly falling snow
Peaceful
We have been waiting for snow
Waiting for the protection
Of the feeling - of snow
A strong barrier
To stop the fray
Between politics of the day
Both in Canada and USA
Enjoying the disappearance
Of angry wrangling
Fear mongering
Threatening pensions
One must work longer to be paid
What politicians have promised
If we are steady Canadians
If we obey
Instead - dreamer's day
Watching twirls of smoke
From fireplace chimneys
Imagining - fragrance of wood burning
Of breakfast cooking
Coffee perking
Smiling - grateful - laughter
For a day away - from worries - tormenting - lamenting
Wishing it would stay
QUIET SNOWY MORNING

RAINY DAY

Sunday, November 27, 2011

As I look out on roofs
From between lightly silvered
Rain drops
Clinging to windows
French doors - of my lighthouse in the sky
Facing - south - west and north
It is a - gray - velvety - quietly - contemplative - scene
Heavy gray clouds
Releasing moisture - gently
There are little lakes
On top of red brick - tall
Victorian houses
Here in Cabbagetown
I imagine people baking
Cookies for Christmas
Plumb puddings
Mince meat pies and tarts
In warm - fragrant - kitchens
Writing gift lists
Blue - white smoke rising from fireplace chimneys
Wondering - wandering - meandering - calculating
How they will pay for them
In this time of
Occupiers - in parks - in tents
Peacefully - protesting - until
The 99% are ousted
From cities around the world
RAINY DAY

RAPTURE

Friday, October 21, 2011

Well here it is again folks
October 21, 2011
Rapture
Apocalypse now?
Mistake in calculations
The final answer?
Are we ready to go?
To get off this world
In a flurry
A frenzie
The mad fanatics
Tell us so
Are we ready for the cataclysmic
Glow?
Family radio
In California
Refuse to talk
Because
Their train to paradise is slow
Because
Today
Friday, October 21, 2011
Is quite normal
As You Know

RED ADMIRAL BUTTERFLY

April 19, 2012

Red Admiral Butterfly
Why are you here so early
Frost is still around
Threatening to destroy - new life
New plantings - tender shoots
You are looking for nectar
In waves of joyous colour
Will my few violets
So small and fragile
Keep you alive?
Will my periwinkles - little blue jewels
The only flowers - in my jungle gardens?
You play hide and seek with me
Darting around my head
Garden - terrace - deck - in the sky
The grey bandit cat - hiding - waiting stealthily
Teasing - revealing his whereabouts - for all birds to see
With amazing - energy - swiftly - beautifully
You are almost full grown
Have travelled many miles
To reach Cabbagetown
I am happy - to see your brilliant colours
My annual callers
I try not to fret
At your demise
Red Admiral
BUTTERFLY

ROUND TABLE

Arts & Letters Club of Toronto - July 8, 2011

Six chairs occupied
One or two - best creative inquiring minds
In Canada - perhaps - time will confirm
One - brilliant investigative journalist
Others of us - some rejected - one isolated naive - namely - me
Listen intently
To - wit - side splitting humour - delightfully delivered
View subtleties - preconceived notions
Displayed on walls - in hearts - passions - revealed
Some understanding - knowing - deceptions
Quality - experience - pretension
In this richly endowed historical
Home away from home - at one time - Group Of Seven
We are there - to share - encouragement - discussion
Or not - depending on - current obsessions
Learning to tell our stories - to those - who would listen
Free our minds of delusions - expectations - burdens
As well as envy - to be forgiven - with generosity of spirit
However shocking - we are human - indoctrinated - prejudices
Respect - for one's opinions - idiosyncrasies
Of which there are many - naturally expected - tolerated
Because - we are artists in our given categories
Summed - L.A.M.P.S.
Respect - communication - refinement
Always main theme - gathering - indelible fingerprints
Potato chips - quaffing - camaraderie
Canadian - carvings - cravings
ROUND TABLE

SISYPHUS SOUP

Friday, February 3, 2012
The Arts & Letters Club of Toronto

We all stood in line
Waiting to be served the soup
Ladled into white bowls
From the huge silver soup pot
By the tall Sisyphus
Using his hands to encourage
The vapours to waft
Up into his realm
Spoons on the side
We viewed the mostly white
Dotted with yellow corn
Green peas
Thick with protein
In perfectly presented
Alignment
Then we wended our ways
To our respective seats
To slurp up - to eat up
At the long wooden tables
In the Great Hall
To be grateful
For
The nourishment
Of
SISYPHUS SOUP
Yum!

SKIER

January 21, 2012

Minus 8 degrees - sunny day
Many shoppers
On Parliament - bundled up
To the eyes
Including myself
Wearing my Beaver hat
Flaps tied down - over my ears
Fur scarf tied snugly - around my neck
Underneath layers of wool
I wear my special silk - ski underwear
Covering top and legs - warm boots
On Carlton Street
A tall excited young man
Walks toward me
Carrying tall yellow skis
'Great day for skiing!,
Smiling broadly - cheerfully - he replies
YES! IT SURE IS! IT SURE IS!
As he strides toward Riverdale Park
For a downhill run - in the sun - fun
Brings back joyous - happy memories
Of my cross country skiing adventures - alone in the
Moraines of Caledon
Barely enough snow this year
Thin layer of snow over ice
This does not stop - the dedicated - Canadian
Breathing - refreshingly - deeply - walker - or
SKIER

SOFT SOLED SLIPPERS

Waiting for us
Welcoming
When we return home
Inside the front door
To slip into - with pleasure
Sensually - sensationally - comfortingly
As we leave off our daily roughness
Aggressive - hard - soled - striding - posturing
To impress - intimidate - those who would interfere
With our - single - minded - purposes
Where we leave
Our hard soled - street - work - boots - shoes
On the mat
Where we enter a quiet - considerate - domain
Our home! - our home! - our home!
We are home!
No one's home - but our own!
Where noisy - pounding - galloping - racing - intrusion
Does not echo through thin walls
On - bare-as-a-bone - wooden - stairs
Where bare wood is respected
Where other's rest is not disturbed
Where we can tread softly
Soothing rest - away from others
Pressing - favours
We are grateful for - our very own home!
As children - some - were taught - the value of
SOFT SOLED SLIPPERS

STORM

August 24, 2011

Night - fiercest storm in memory
Thunder trembled
The earth
Loud - roiling - threatening
Lightning - intruded - penetrating - windows - mirrors
Doors - ceilings - walls - floors
Lingering
Long - jagged - fat ropes - skeletal fingers
Veins in belly of sky - delivering - birth of storm
Bursting - attacking - CNTower - thrusting - blinking
Striking hundreds of times
Our world
As far as we could see
Sky lighted ominously
Wind - rain - pounding
My skylights
Red bricks shuddering
While I watched - with amazement - awe
Tried not to be frightened
Planned what I would take with me to basement
There were tornado warnings
In Toronto
Advice on how to prepare
For survival of fiercest - in memory
STORM

SUMMER IN CABBAGETOWN

July 17, 2011

Hot - humidity warning
Air conditioners blasting
Rumbling - rocking
Sidewalks steaming - tar melting
Sun beating down
Lounging - reading 'the art of seduction'
In my cool green jungle garden - soft breeze
On Sackville Street
Wafting laughter - music - bottles - caps - clinking - clanking
Reaches me from garden parties
Deck parties - swimming pools
Under gay umbrellas
North - south - east - west
Cabbagetowners - relaxing rules
Indulging in tales of woe
Adventures - growing
In animated retelling
Friendships forming
Animosities - foreboding
Dressed their best
Panama - Tilley hats - large straw with ribbons
Short gowns - sandals - bare skin glowing
Tots riding kiddy cars
On way to Riverdale Farm
People posing - photographically
Ice cream cones - dripping
From sticky fingers

Happy - sticky - cheeks
Bright eyes - calculating
Time for next seduction
Birds - squirrels lurking - for party food - droppings
Dogs barking
On Parliament Street
Outdoor cafes - crowded
Beer quaffing - camaraderie
A police siren - stuns to silence
Who got out of hand?
On hot day in summer
At parties
SUMMER IN CABBAGETOWN

SYMMETRY

LOVE

Design of love
Lines
Foldings
Find the centre
To find foldings
Numbers
Times
To make life seem
SYMMETRICAL
Unseen dimensions
Waves - intrusions
Lengths - Longings
Spaces - Projected
Interjected
Corners - Turned
Conclusions
Indecisive
Lack of understanding
Set patterns
Difficult to navigate
With angry people
Whose SYMMETRY has been entangled
In religious dogma
Keep searching
For
SYMMETRY
LOVE

TEMPO ADAGIO

Woo me slowly Monsieur
There is no need to rush
I am willing
If you play me intriguingly - slowly
Meaningfully
With passion
With subtlety
With tenderness
With charm - laughter
Music - deep bass to tinkling treble
Tempo Adagio
Please
We are a skating pair
I am here - you are there
Spinning circles
With perfection of form
Now you may lift me
A ballet of grace - beauty
Un adagio - sil vous plea Monsieur
Our acrobatic formations
Will be graceful
Completely rounded - accomplished
Delicate - yet strong - with experience
Entice me
To surrender to your strength
With gentleness
Avec la Douceur - Monsieur
TEMPO ADAGIO

'THE CONTAINED GARDEN'

'Beautiful small gardens in downtown Toronto'
April 27, 2012

Yes! I will have gardeners - this spring!
They are - 'The Contained Garden'
Karen and Jim / greenthumbs
Knowledgeable - caring - kind - design conscious
Exactly what I needed - for my small sanctuary
My jungle garden - healing - green - walled - borders
For birds to bathe - in the small pond - chattering - songs
Butterflies - to tease - swooping - merrily
Visiting opossum - to sip
Visiting raccoons - to wash paws - while cavorting
Squirrels to romp - waggling tails - begging food
Visiting cats of all colours - to hide - to sip - softly
Beautified - vine covered walls - softening - privacy
Today - all in my garden are happy
A pair of cardinals - in seduction - viewing themselves
Flapping wings - spreading - jewels of water drops
Sparrows - finding crumbs - on swept brick floors
Not having to jump - dig - in last autumn's leaves
Dancing amongst - cascaded lilly of the valley
Clumps of purple violets
Carpet - for dreaming - inspiration - lounge
Under Honey Locust - Cedar trees - Weeping Cyprus
Honey Suckle
I am grateful for my
Contained Gardeners
'THE CONTAINED GARDEN'

THE DAY AFTER THE "RAPTURE"

May 22, 2011

Awoke this morning
With a smile on my face
The world did not end
As the fanatically obsessed - religious
Doomsdayers
Predicted
I am still here - my friends are still here
We remained on the job
Did not liquidate our assets
Still have a roof over our heads
Can still laugh - cry - sing - dance
Make love
So lets have a party!
Lets raise a flag of celebration
From the CNTower
Pop a few corks
And try to solve some difficult
Problems facing our planet
Pity the doomsdayers
Who must try to put their lives back together
Again
&
Again - Again - Again

Cheers! for

THE DAY AFTER THE "RAPTURE"
For Karen and Jim / Greenthumbs

"THE IRISH GENTLEMAN"

DECEMBER 25, 2011
For Brian Hill et al

Invitation
By telephone
"I am cooking a turkey
For a gathering of friends
Would like you to be with us"
His masculine voice
Mellow and kind
From the handsome "Jock - Ironman" I had met
'At the House On Parliament'
Perhaps seven years ago
While sharing conversation - with a cigarette
The only ones on the patio
On a very cold - damp day
Then in Cabbagetown
Several times - while walking his "dogies"
We kept in touch via email - throughout the years
His love of dogs - impressed me very much
I love dogs - they seem to like me
Entering his home
I was greeted by - delicious aromas
Of a twenty-five pound turkey being cooked to perfection
With all the trimmings - including divine mashed potatoes
Four lovely well behaved - amusing - "doggie" conversations
In barking mode - nuzzling
Stirred my emotions from: Albert - Jasper - Kurt - Bengy
All males

"I am comfortable in the company of males"
As well as his charming guests - Jenn (Jeff) whom I had met
At the Cabbagetown Fall Festival
When the "Irish Gentleman" had invited me
For a drink with his friends - plus live jazz music
At the 'House On Parliament Street' Cafe
Much fun - laughter - singing
We drank his heady - deep full bodied - rich red wine
Which he had made at 'The Wine Rack' on Parliament Street
Loosening our creative thoughts and tongues
Ate his completely spectacular dinner
Shared rich conversation - our concerns - experiences
Past and present - photos of himself (in a bikini on a beach'
His parents wedding photo - plus ex's
While charming - 'Bob Mickleboro' trained his camera on us
Ease - comfortable - interesting - learning
Laughter - bright - intelligent
The 'Taurus Tiger' - Jenn (Jeff)
And myself had a common bond
I being a Taurean as well
He read my poem 'Four River Songs of My Life'
From my poetry book 'Rooted in Cabbagetown'
Read it so well!
In this company there was no tension - no anger
Only a freedom of expression - knowledge
Joyous sharing - fun!
Giving thanks for
A memorable
Christmas Dinner - prepared by the perfect host
Never to be forgotten! B.H.!
THE "IRISH GENTLEMAN"

THE RAPTURED

MAY 21, 2010

Twenty million Christian souls
Expected to ascend into heaven
Quit their jobs
Sold all their possessions
Expecting to be lifted into the heavens
Eternally
I, on the other hand
Have lived in a state of rapture
All of my life
Enraptured by beauty
In all its forms
Music which transcends - mesmerizes - enraptures me
My little jungle pond - fountain - rhythmically - hauntingly
Joyous - sparkling water of life
Flowing
Singing its forever song
Birds singing their eternal song
A deep masculine voice - calling my name
An expansive vista
Sparkling - loving eyes - knowingly - caring
Pianos played with passion
Is it possible that
I ascended to heaven at my birth?
Even at conception?
Was the date of my enrapturement
May 13th?
Because I remain
THE RAPTURED

TURKEYS

Thanksgiving 2011

Turkeys are perkey
When all fluffed up
To display - their beauty - colourful plumage
The great tail fan - with enormous span
The gobble - garbled voice - to make us laugh
We look closely
At their strange red waddle
A beak - so unbelievable
A nose so unlike our own - except the popes
Not embarrassed - I am a 50 pounder - proud of it
They do not know their fate
To be slowly cooked in an oven at 55 degrees
Until they are golden brown - from basting - in their juices
To be served - all plucked - stuffed with bread - sausage
Nuts - raisins - remains of fridges and cupboards
To be carved up - divvied up
For our dinner plates
With gravy - mashed potatoes
Squash - sweet potatoes
Snow peas - cranberries
Their final mates
As we scrape our plates
Take their wish bone - imagined - wishes for
Dry them up
To be pulled apart by pinkies - gambling to win
649 Lottery
TURKEYS

URIM AND THUMMIN

Lux et Veritas
Light and Truth discovery in words
{Crystals and gems used as casting lots or stones
to speak to gods}

I cast my crystals and gems
By way of words
Formed into lines of poetry
A way of discovery
Into nature's mysteries
Into my own inner nature
Looking for connections
Communing
With expression
To enliven
A blank page
So that others may
Understand
My peculiarities
In the embellished crime
of
Poetry
URIM AND THUMMIN
Lux et Veritas

VENUS MY RULING PLANET

March 5, 2012

Good morning Venus
My ruling planet
Welcome back
To this
Most important day
Giving light and love
To the world
Of Quantum Fields
Many dimensions
Explorations
Indications
Communications
We have been waiting
For your arrival
So that we may - once more - thrive
For all that has been building
Since your last departure
We await your rapture
A massive
Boost to our adventure
Good morning
VENUS
I toast you with - fresh spinach - garlic soup
Sweet red apple - maple syrup
Good morning
VENUS
MY RULING PLANET

WEST WING

Cold west wind blows through
West wing - on second floor - behind door
Where forgotten memories are stored
With each objet d'art
Creations
Dreams
Flow in streams
In cold darkness
Of west wing
Seen by only a few - unscroupulous looters
Drapery flutters at icy windowpane
Possibilities
Waiting to be renewed - in spring
Walls bare of insulation
Remain in isolation
Echoes
Of past ambitions
Haunting - energies - abounded - in anticipation
Skillful hands
Applying ancient perceptions
New inventions
To their times - places
Now shivering
As
Cold west wind blows through
Second floor
WEST WING

WHEN VARIATIONS GO ASTRAY

February 5, 2012
Lucky Year of the Dragon

Variations on a theme - the dreamers - dream
When variations
Become a scheme
When variations
Become lost in darkness - lies - deception
In confusion - others meddling - intrusion
When variations
Become twisted - lost in the wind of lust - desire
When blinding assumptions - presumptions
In the labyrinth
Of egos - quest for gold - soul - sold
Power struggles
The themes
Of music - poetry - love
Become a drudgery
When variations - scream the sour note
To float - as envy - jealousy - greed
When variations - barren cupboard - of the heart
Has no nourishment to display
Become - a mockery - broken trust
It is time to find the thrust
The original path
Pull back - gather in - resources - courage
Direct your dedication
Look at your compass
How could it go so wrong?

Where did we turn the wrong way?
Noble thoughts - creating - beauty
Democracy - Ethics - Integrity
Fun - joy - play - innocence
Find the true north star
The load star - pole star
Tie a wish - thread knot - to its inspiration
Illumination
Polaris
See it beaming - guiding - listening - magnetizing
Lighting the way
WHEN VARIATIONS GO ASTRAY

WOBBLY TOOTH

Was this wobbly tooth
Reflecting
Life around me?
Telling me - be careful
Be mindful of what you eat
What you say
What others - do - say
Have respect - for a wobbly tooth's intuition
Its departure - I put off - for months
Not wishing to have it extracted - leave a space
By a torture inflicting - unknown dentist - apprentice
As I sat dunking a piece of bread
Soaking it in milk - then sucking on it
For nourishment - longing for steak
Until I forgot - chomped down - felt the pain
Pounds began to melt away
Clothes became larger
Grocery bill - smaller
Saving up for - a new tooth installer
Almost overnight
New wardrobe in sight
The expense - a fright
Final - resolution
Let this wobbly tooth - go - its own way
Let the tooth fairy have it - for wobbly tooth heaven
Another life lesson
From - of all things - a
WOBBLY TOOTH

L'ECRITURE DE LA POESIE EST
LA LIBERTE
LA MUSIQUE, LE RHYTHME, LA JOIE!
'Writing poetry is freedom, music, rhythm, joy!'
Barbara Elizabeth Mercer, 2010

LILY OF THE VALLEY MUGUET

Un brin de muguet le premier
mai vous apportera du bonheur toute l'annee.

'A sprig of lily of the valley on May first
will bring you happiness all year long.'
Will gladden your heart with song
Its perfume will lighten your spirit
Will give your troubles respite
Will fill you with delight
A carpet of muguet
Will let you sleep at night
Dream sweet dreams
Bring moon beams
Forgetting all schemes
Will enchant your garden
I am grateful for
My magic garden carpet
Of
LILY OF THE VALLEY
MUGUET

PURPOSEFUL ROBIN

May 1st, 2012

Large Robin
Full throbbing red breast
Searching
Freshly raked earth
Amongst
Richly - fluorescent - translucent - green
Tall leaves of - Lilly of The Valley
Beginning to bud
Tugging - pulling - with all his might
To fill his beak
With nesting - house building
Twigs - roots
As large as half his body
Flies off in northerly direction
A deception - of course
So that other watchers - including me
Are fooled as to the whereabouts
Of his construction site
Stores his loot
Then - makes a show
Flying low - in the opposite direction
For protection
So as to detract
From the fact
He is a
PURPOSEFUL ROBIN

SNAIL LOVE DARTS

May 14, 2012

Early this morning
While retrieving newspaper
From front doorstep
After a sudden down pouring of rain
An amazing - delightful event - snails
Covering only my sidewalk
Had it rained snails?
Could it be they were trying to make contact
With each other - with me
With their love darts?
Their mating courtship
Yes - I looked them up
Snail mythology
They have a love dart
Shaped like a spear
They try to imbed the dart in
Prospective amours
By shooting a dart or arrow
So that they will have offspring
Wanting to protect them
From being trod on
I plucked each one
Placing them in
Moist Periwinkle - carpeted garden
Amidst the blue jewel blossoms
A proper place for courtship
To shoot
SNAIL LOVE DARTS

Guest Poet
Lucy Brennan

Idyll

Outdoors
in a little courtyard
they are playing a Boccherini minuet.

We are seated, not touching.

Notes fall,
leaves lift in a soft breeze . . .
The skirts of the shadow-dancers swirl.

Tea Trays

China cups
lace doilies
cucumber sandwiches
and
great grandmothers
holding the past
in the tips of their fingers

Lucy Brennan
Author, Poet
R.C. Mercer
Feb. 2012

Keron D. Platt

Youth; The Artist

I take a brush
to the canvas and liberate
a space
in which I project my solitude
With dauntless stroke
I fire a glow
in the heart of my soul
Dreams and fantacies
invade on the fringe
of creation
announcing a discovery
of an unknown continent -
the capture
of the instantaneous
Points of view shift
re-arranging the visual field
In time an idea explodes
into wild colours and
I acquire my independence

KERON P. PLATT
AUTHOR POET

Leon Warmski

Untitled

I will have
The one more day
before the car
takes me away
to see my lady fair
sitting in the cafe chair
along the Blod. du Montparnasse,
I will walk the pavement here
and the Cafe will be there;
and have one more drink-
the coffee strong, black as ink
and see the green busses of the Metro
go-
either fast or slow
Yes, I will have
the one more day
to go back to that Cafe!
Then I awake and blink.
DAMN;
It was all a dream
I think? -